Teach Me Writing

Handwriting and learning to read go together

Handwriting practice book

A companion book to
the Reading Lesson

Teach Me Writing

Michael Levin and Charan Langton

Mountcastle Company
www.readinglesson.com
Email: support@readinglesson.com

Print ISBN 978-0-913063-23-1
Library of Congress Catalog Card Number 99-64110

Art work by
Barbara Zeiring

August 2021

A few words...

Let's improve your child's reading skills with handwriting.

Children learn reading faster and easier if they learn it together with handwriting. Our brain memorizes the shape of the letters from direct messages coming from the fingers and wrist joints. Writing exercises build strong connection between the sound and shape of the letter, and that leads to reading fluency.

Teach Me Handwriting is a companion book that follows the lessons in ***The Reading Lesson*** book. In this book, your child will be tracing the grayed-out letters. Ask her to copy the letters and words in the blank space next to the grayed-out words. She can also color the pictures. There is a story at the end of each lesson that she can either copy from ***The Reading Lesson*** book or write her own.

If your child is under the age of five, you may want to also try the **ABC Writing Lesson** book. **ABC Writing Lesson** book is developmentally-appropirate for a younger child. It is in color and helps child learn to trace and write letters and numbers on clean and uncluttered pages.

Try not to be rigid about the way your child forms the letters. Every child has a unique writing style and follows own path of fine motor development. Slowly, she will develop an individual handwriting style and, over time, will become better at it. Be patient. Only practice and repetition matter at this point.

If you need additional pages for practice, you may find them in an expanded version of this book, in printable format, available on our website.

On our website, we have little lcertificates, one for each lesson. After your child completes a lesson, download and print out the certificate. Let your child redeem these certificates for a special toy or treat. Also remember to save this book after he is done. It makes a wonderful memory keepsake.

Giggle Bunny wishes you happy reading and writing.

Charan Langton
Michael Levin

Lesson 1

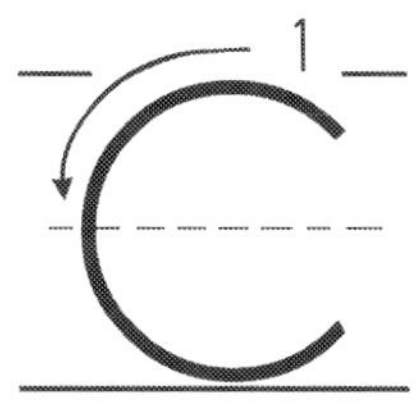
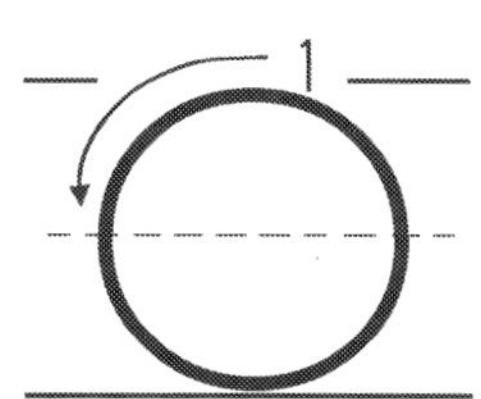
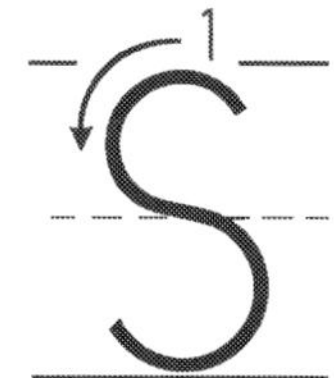
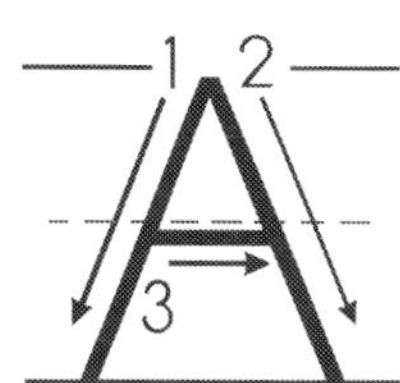
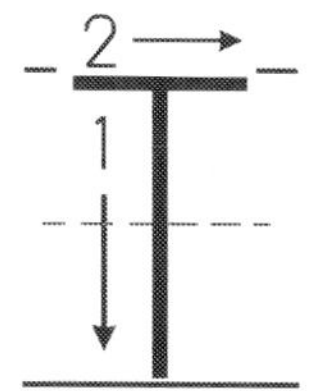

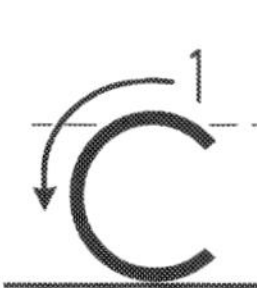
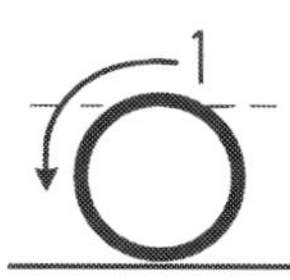

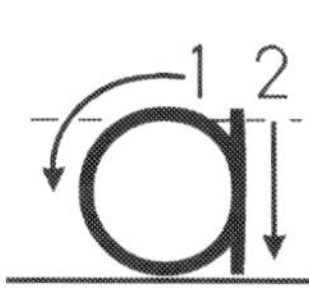
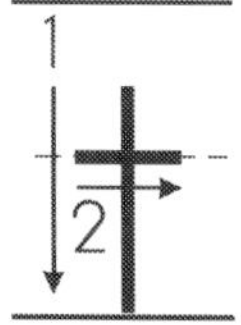

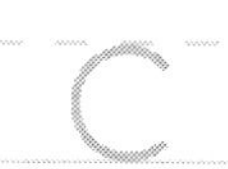

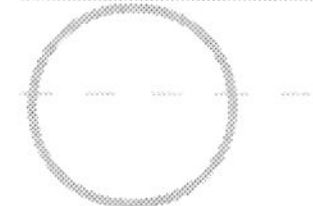
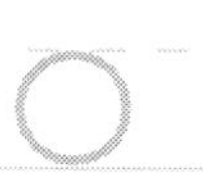
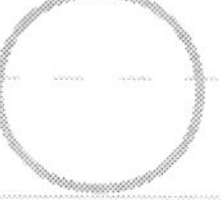
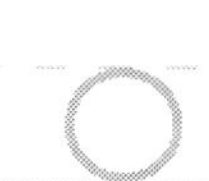
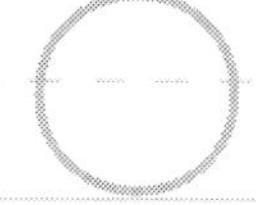
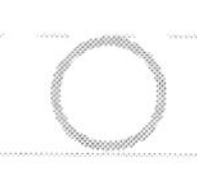

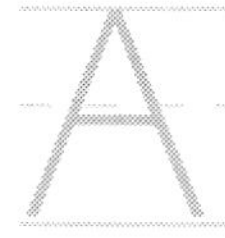
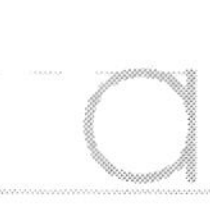
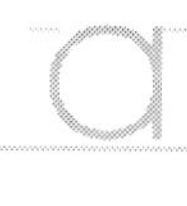

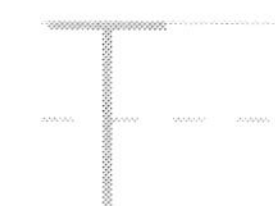

Trace the letter.

c c c c c c

o o o o o o

s s s s s s

a a a a a a

t t t t t t

T t T t T t

A A a A a A

S S s S s S

C c C c C c

T t T t T t

Trace the word and copy.

at

cat

sat

cot

a cat

sat

cat

cot

My story

Ask your child to copy the story from The Reading Lesson book or make her own. Also, let's color the picture.

Lesson 2

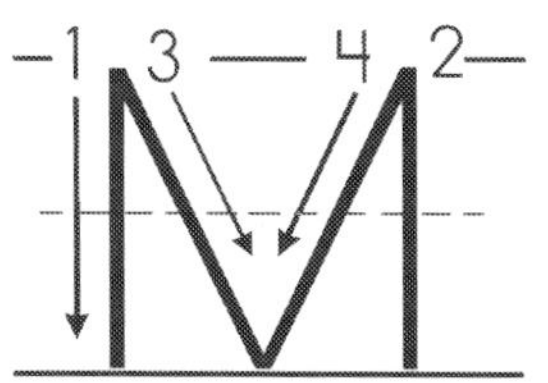

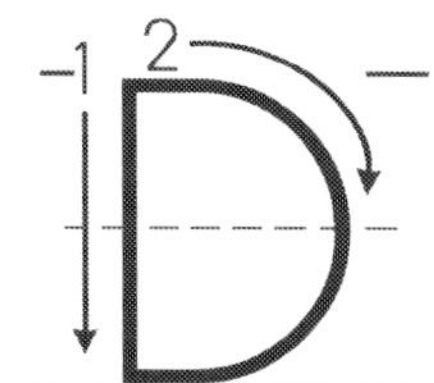

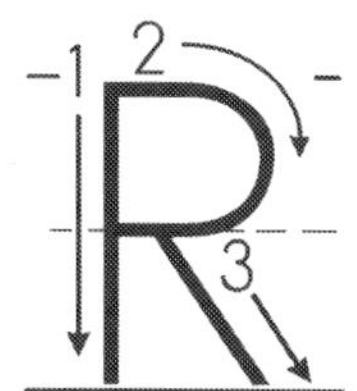

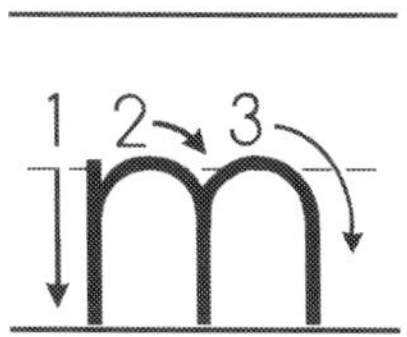

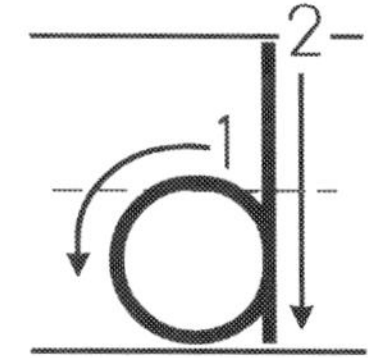

M m M m M m

D d D d D d

R r R r R r

A a A a A a

S s S s S s

O o O o O o

Trace and then copy

m m m m m m

d d d d d d

r r r r r r

a a a a a a

s s s s s s

M m M m M m

A a A a A a

R r R r R r

D d D d D d

T t T t T t

Trace and then copy

rat

mat

sat

dot

sad

dot

mad

Sat

Trace and then copy

At

at

Mat

sat

Rat

sad

am

mad

rod

rat

Trace and then copy

At

A cat

A rat

rat sat

sad

rat

am

mad

Cat

My story

Ask your child to copy the story from The Reading Lesson book or make her own. Also, let's color the picture.

Lesson 3

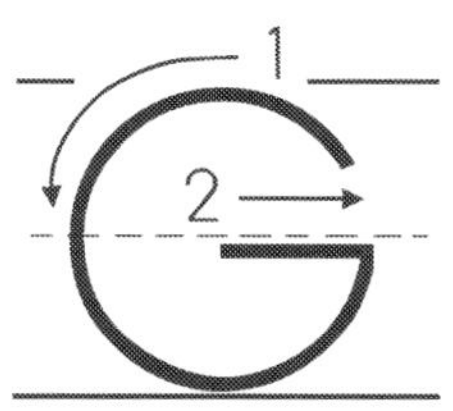
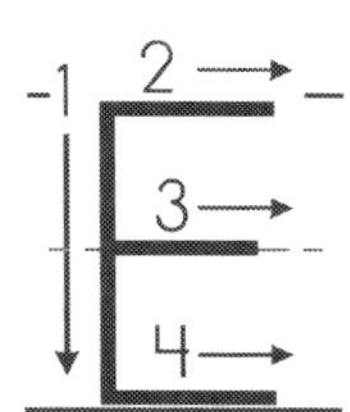
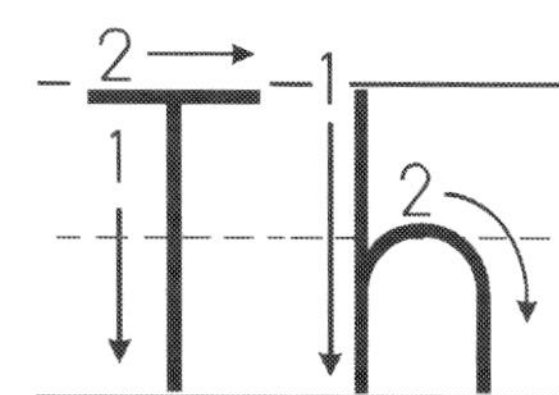

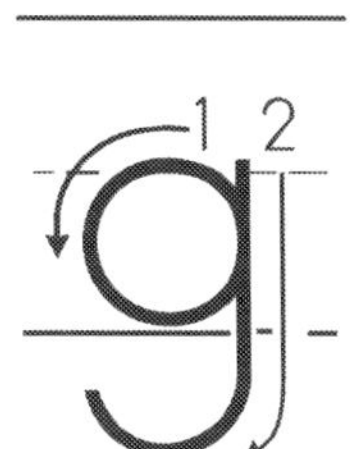
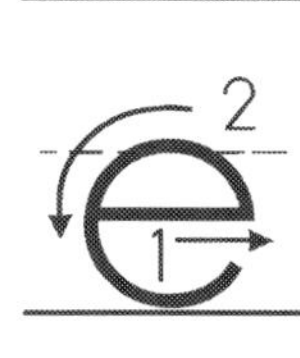
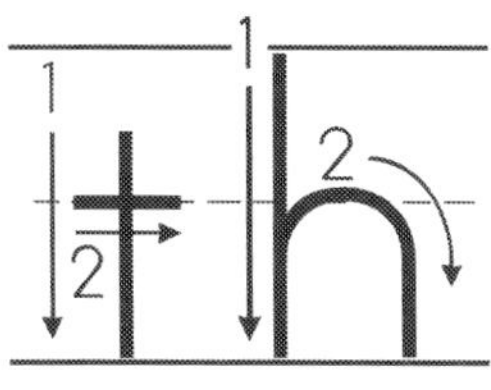

G g G g G g

E e E e E e

T t T t T t

Th th Th th Th th

M m M m M m

A a A a A a

g g g

e e e

m m m

r r r

th th th

G g G g G g

E e E e E e

M m M m M m

A a A a A a

Th th Th th Th th

met

got

set

get

got

red

egg

rag

get

met

cot

got

rag

sag

red

rod

rot

the cat

the dog

get cat

got it

the rag

the mat

met cat

set it

mad cat

My story

Ask your child to copy the story from The Reading Lesson book or make her own. Also, let's color the picture.

Lesson 4

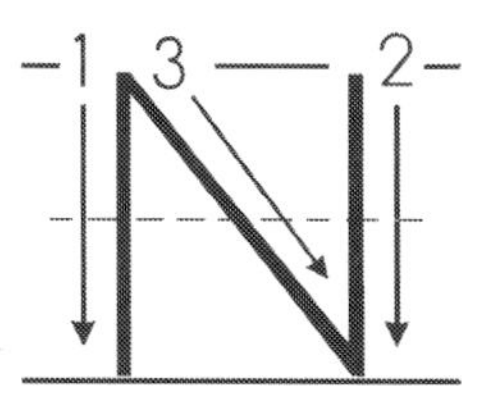

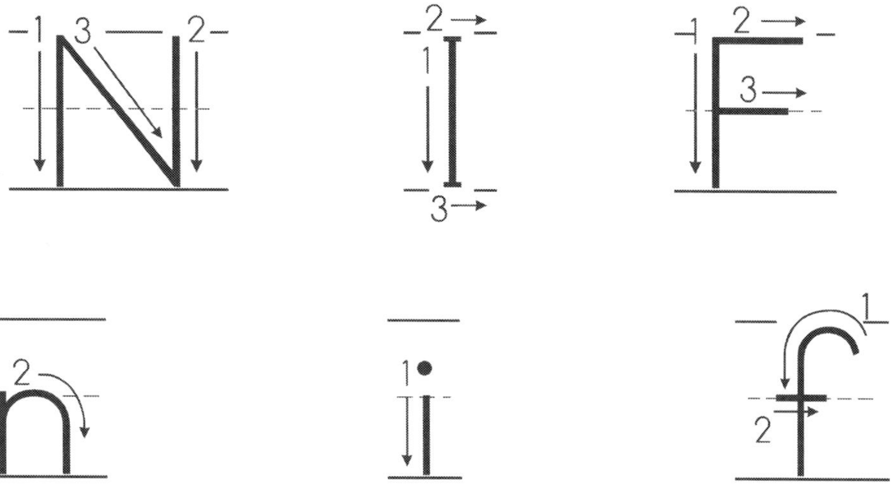

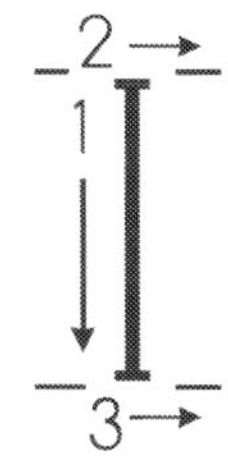

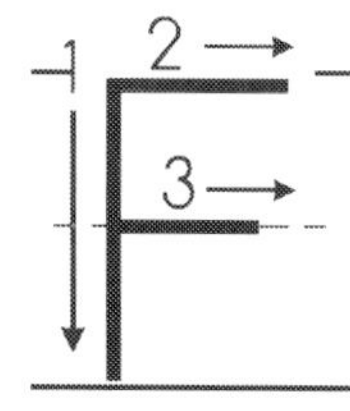

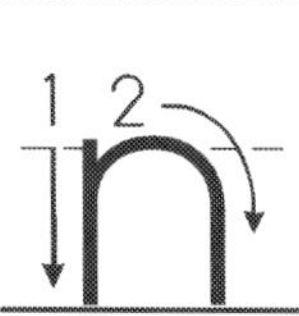

1 i

1
f
2

N n N n N n

I i I i I i

F f F f F f

G g G g G g

E e E e E e

T t T t T t

Trace and then copy

Lesson 4

n n n

i i i

f f f

a a a

h h h

N n N n N n

E e E e E e

F f F f F f

M m M m M m

T t T t T t

tan

ran

fan

Fit

got

not

Dot

did

ran

it fit

fan

dot

not in

and

sand

tag it

rag

Trace and then copy

it is

in it

on it

This is

That is

in can

sand

not in

the dot

My story

Ask your child to copy the story from The Reading Lesson book or make her own. Also, let's color the picture.

Lesson 5

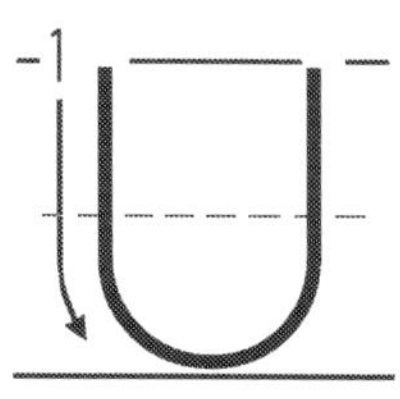

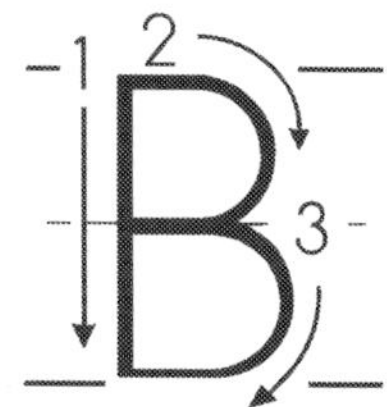

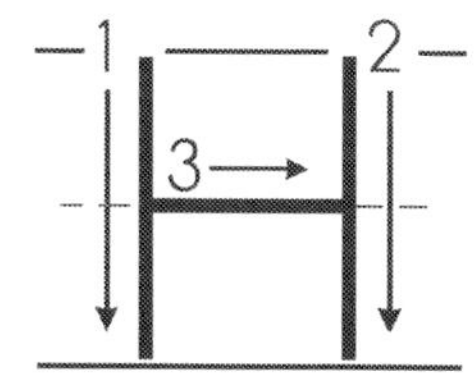

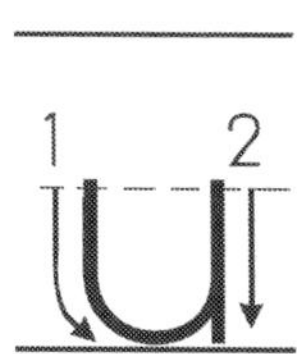

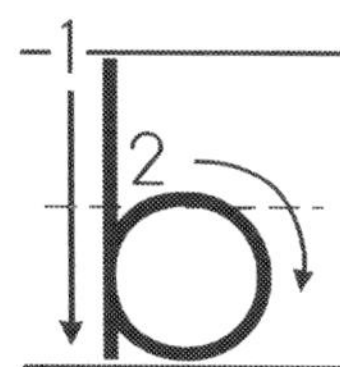

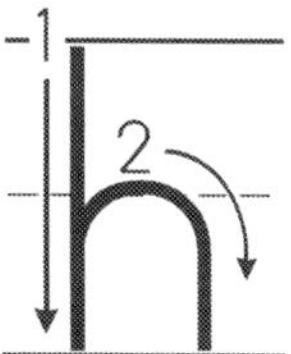

U u U u U u

B b B b B b

H h H h H h

G g G g G g

d b d b d b

D d D d D d

b d b d b d b

d d

b b

d d

b b

bus

but

has

hen

not

ban

bad

bag

dad

b d

dog

beg

bet

bed

Big bus

Big hat

Man ran.

it is gone

it is done

This hat

That is it.

Red bed

Dog ran.

It is

I got it.

Bob is in.

Did it.

Tom ran.

Ten men.

That man

This bed

Red can.

My story

Ask your child to copy the story from The Reading Lesson book or make her own. Also, let's color the picture.

Lesson 6

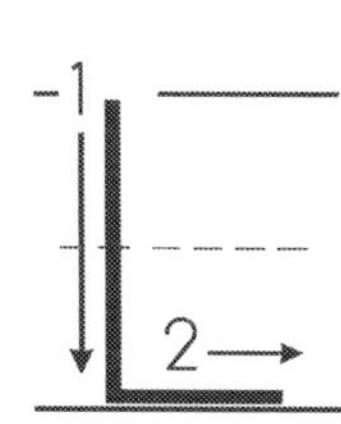

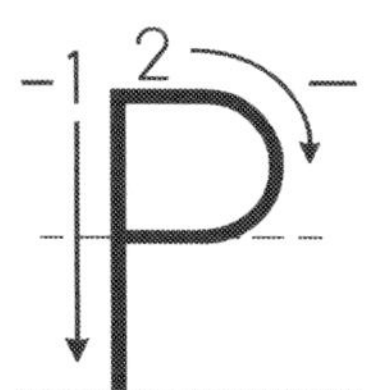

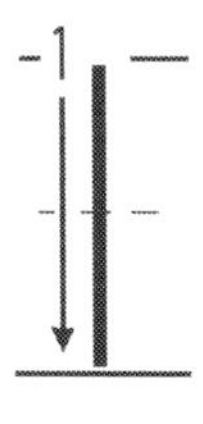

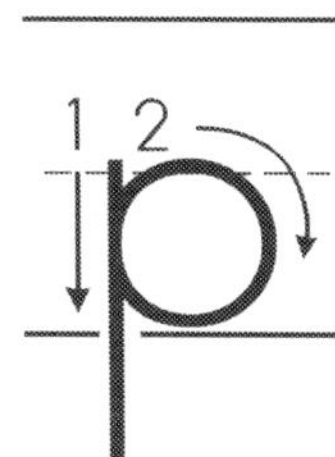

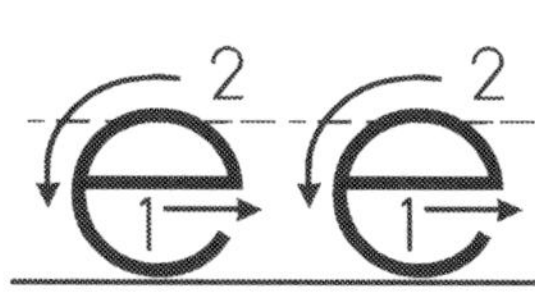

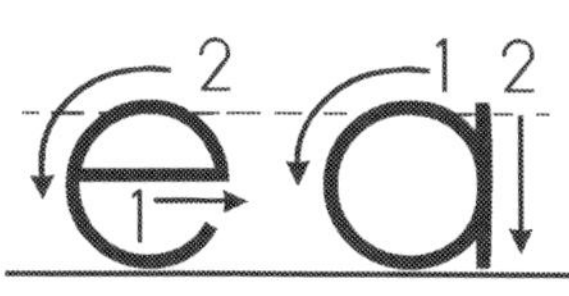

L l L l L l

P p P p P p

E e E e E e

ee ea ee ea ee ea

B b B b B b

D d D d D d

he

me

bee

see

let

lot

up

tell

little

bell

Trace and then copy

Call up

tell me

Read

See me

feet

feed

seed

need

Big bee

Neat

it is near

the heat

her feet

big sea

Tell me

big pot

Red pen

Trace and then copy

eats bugs

Duck is in.

run hen

red hat

bed back

Little

not big

has fun

in the sun

My story

Lesson 7

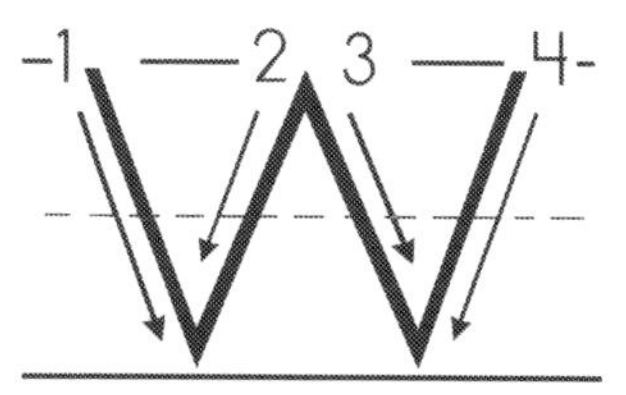

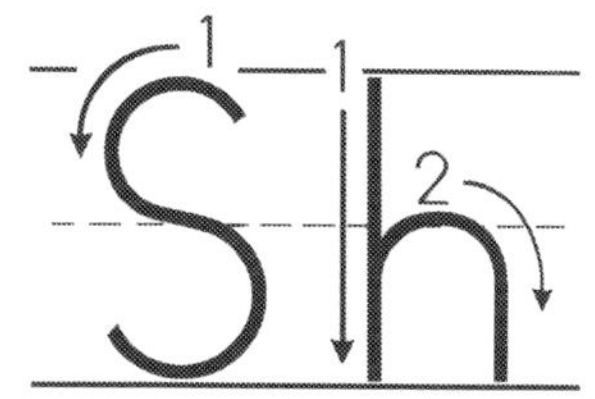

1 sh 1 2

W w W w W w

Sh sh Sh sh Sh sh

P p P p P p

E e E e E e

ea ee ea ee ea ee

N n N n N n

we

wet

well

shop

ship

will

well

them

there

want

Trace and then copy

pet

let

sell

bell

all

tall

wall

ball

There
with me
it was
we were
we said

We went
small ball
wet wall
then
them

He will win.

Let it be.

She said

Lots of

He left

So small

Little ball

Fish shop

we went

Tall wall

Little bit

My story

Lesson 8

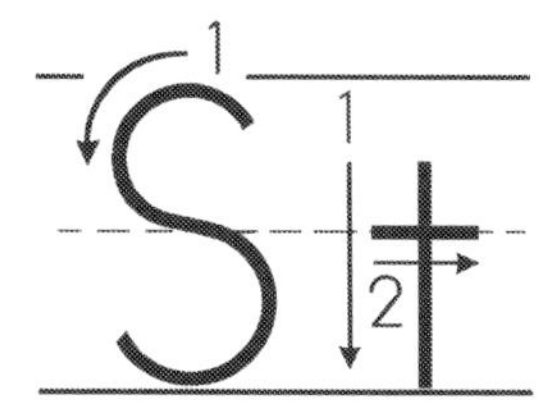

st

W w W w W w

St st St st St st

M m M m M m

N n N n N n

H h H h H h

U u U u U u

St

Stop

Step

shop

said

hi

tie

lie

fine

nine

ride

pipe

time

pine

stop

wife

fast

best

must

pin pine

fin fine

hid hide

sit site

bit bite

win wine

rid ride

tin tine

mit mite

dim dime

I am big.

I can read.

She reads.

I swim.

I tell time.

That tree

Little ball

It is time.

Did it well.

Need it

Pet shop

My story

Lesson 9

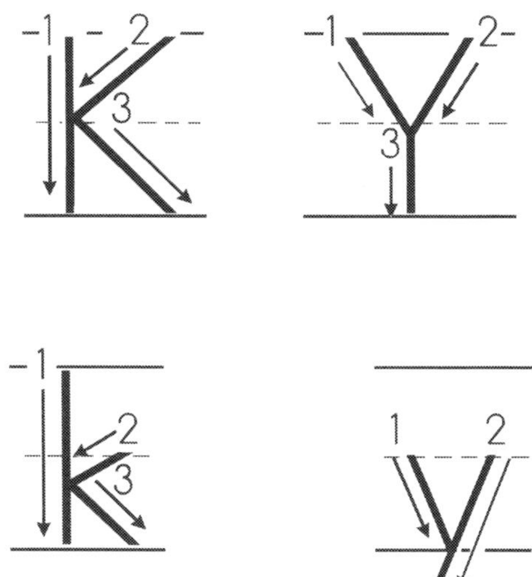

K k K k K k

Y y Y y Y y

Sh sh Sh sh Sh sh

St st St st St st

H h H h H h

U u U u U u

are

you

sleep

can

You

Kids

like

bikes

star

from

Trace and then copy

cart

park

dark

bark

barn

farm

black

block

You and I

I am fine.

Stop that.

You will

sleep well

with you

with me

best pal

from

kitten

I sleep.

You read.

She reads.

You and I

I got help.

It is warm.

It is dark.

I like stars.

near farm

walk

talk

My story

Lesson 10

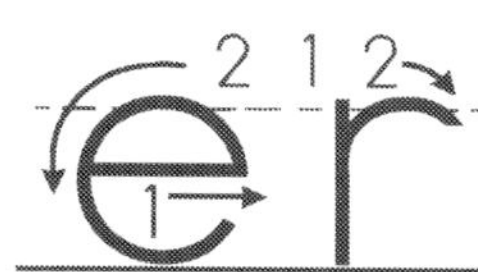

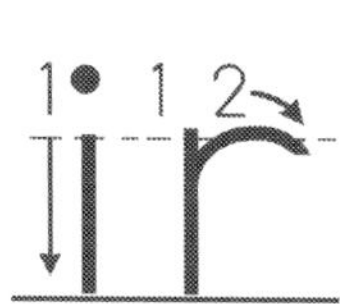

K k K k K k

ur ur ur ur ur ur

ir ir ir ir ir ir

Ar ar Ar ar Ar ar

To to To to To to

er er er er er er

Trace and then copy

bird

your

her

were

after

turn

burn

girl

your

sister

brother

mother

father

mister

water

farm

hard

taller

darker

Your car

Stop that.

Bigger

Butter

faster

better

biggest

got you

girls

Black bird

come here

from it

and her

stir tea

friend

come back

eaters

kind mind

sweet

sweeter

My story

Lesson 11

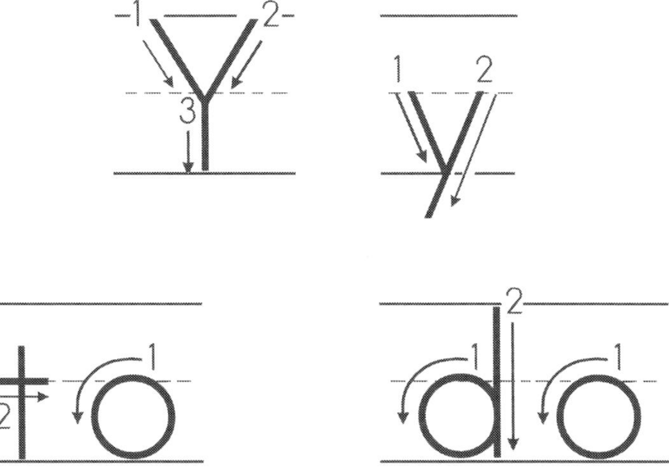

Y y Y y Y y

to to to to to to

do do do do do do

Go go Go go Go go

Do do Do do Do do

Er er Er er Er er

Trace and then copy

Do

you

yell

my

sky

buy

tool

food

boom

boot

pool

soon

spoop

stool

shook

goop

moon

stood

good book

Your car

look good

stood up

You first

look here

cook book

My room

Try a fry

Please

Trace and then copy

she looks

good bye

shirt

after

together

doctor

friend

good girl

red wood

Try to do

I went far.

My story

Lesson 12

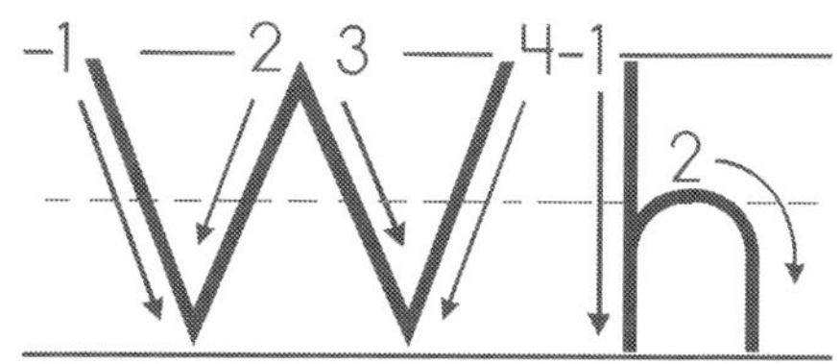

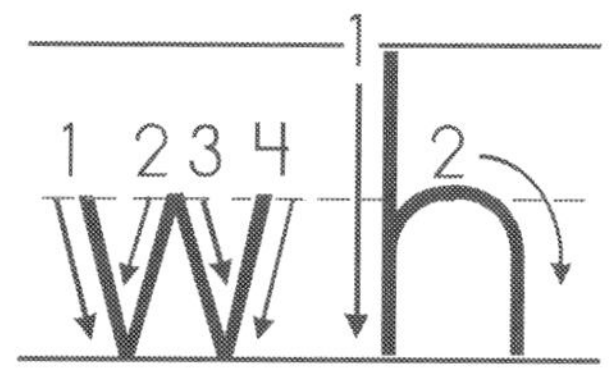

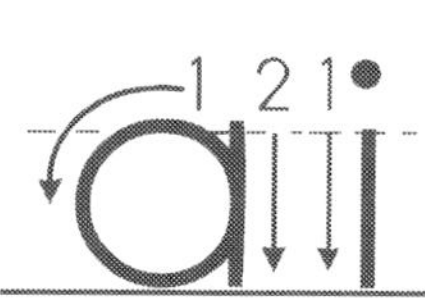

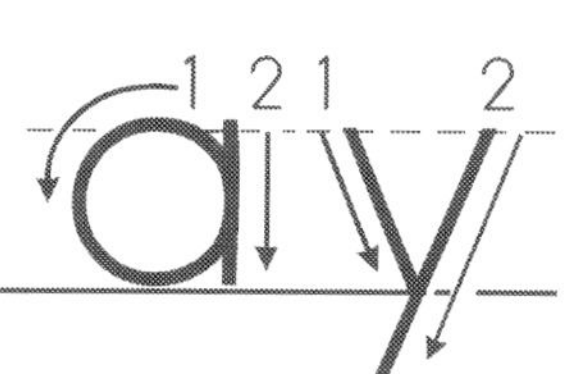

Oo oo Oo oo Oo oo

ai ai ai ai ai ai

No no No no No no

ay ay ay ay ay ay

wh wh wh wh wh wh

Wh Wh Wh Wh

Trace and then copy

way

when

where

what

white

may

bay

whale

state

paper

Trace and then copy

does

today

Real

pray

rain

hair

Day

Bay

Ray

Say

May

Trace and then copy

Monday

Sunday

Friday

days

air

fair

mail

nail

Trace and then copy

cap cape

rat rate

mad made

tap tape

hat hate

mat mate

Sam same

pan pane

can cane

fat fate

bat bate

at ate

My story

Lesson 13

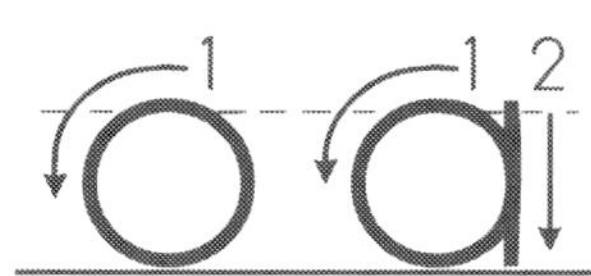

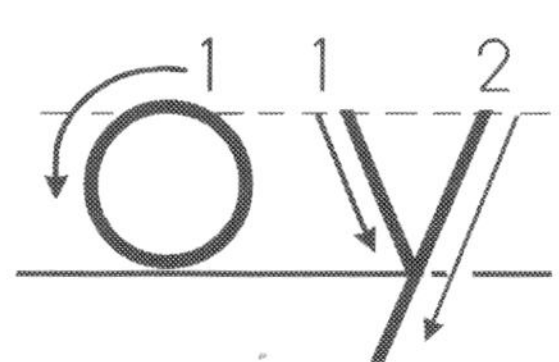

oa oa oa oa oa

ow ow ow ow ow

Go go Go go Go

oy oy oy oy oy

Th Th Th Th Th

Wh wh Wh wh

Boy

Toy

sold

sold gold

old coat

bow

tow

more

Store

Those

oak tree

Go away.

Go home.

Old man

wide road

Take soap.

small fish

big fish

little boat

Dig a hole.

In the sea

coat

toad

road

oak

bow

row

yellow

window

Trace and then copy

not note

hop hope

cop cope

rob robe

ton tone

dot dote

pop pope

cod code

rod rode

dom dome

rot rotten

man mane

My story

Lesson 14

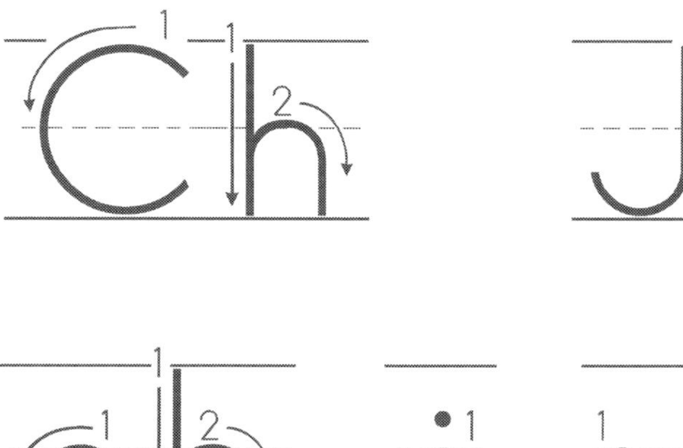

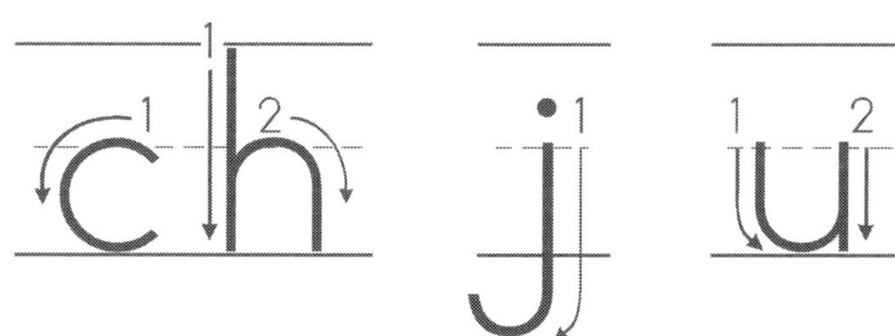

Ch ch Ch ch Ch ch

J j J j J j

U u U u U u

ay ai ay ai ay ai

ue ue ue ue ue ue

Jean Jen John Jack

Use

used

tunes

cubes

tubes

Duke

dune

just

June

jam

Trace and then copy

so cute

John

Jill

jet

Music

just

open

train

true blue

blue glue

Sue or Jane

pull pulled

chop

chat

rich

much

such

chin

catch

Catch it.

Pull it.

use nails

Match it.

cuckoo

play chess

teacher

good job

yellow chick

each other

red, white

and blue

My story

Lesson 15

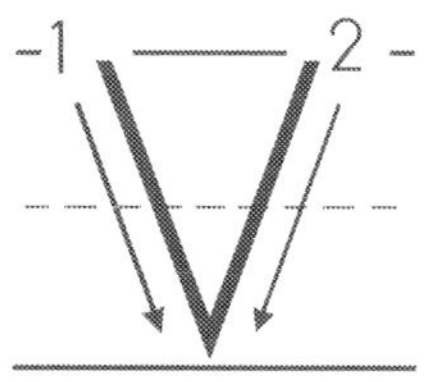

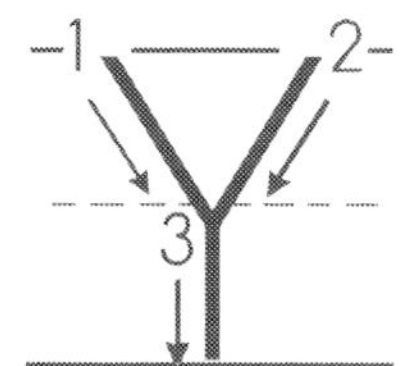

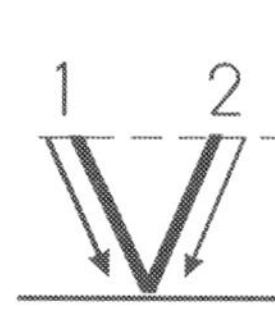

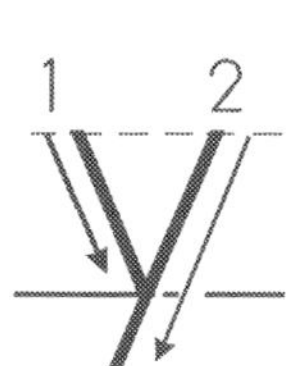

V v V v V v

J j J j J j

Y y Y y Y y

ch ue re ar ir ch

my by ry fy by ny

Yes No yes no

Trace and then copy

Love

have

live

give

any

many

only

very

money

save

Sunny day

Funny boy

Dog barks.

never

every

puppy

tiny

many

Trace and then copy

Rainy day

tiny key

give me

Very dirty

Pretty

honey

mommy

daddy

again

which

much

I gave it.

have fun

We have it.

Mary

Billy

funny story

empty jar

So happy

Really good

very funny

visit me

yellow vest

My story

Lesson 16

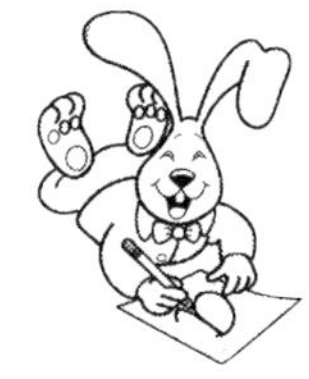

1 X 2   1 Z

1 x 2   1 z

X x X x X x

Z z Z z Z z

V v V v V v

ch sh ch sh ch sh

oy oa oy oa oy oa

sp st sp st sp st

Mix it.

Zap it.

zero

zebra

box

fixed

mixed

zoo

Exit

text

Trace and then copy

Mexico

fixed

Buzz

zip

zipper

sister

every

very

train track

blue blimp

speak

I love her.

every tree

speed

It is over.

Done, gone

again

Exit

Zoo

Trace and then copy

one, two

three, four

five, six

seven, eight

nine, ten

zero

numbers

pushed

Rabbit

Six foxes

Max

Taxi

My story

Lesson 17

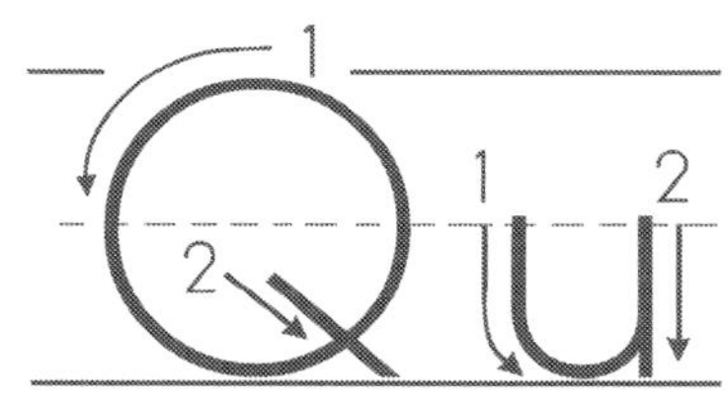

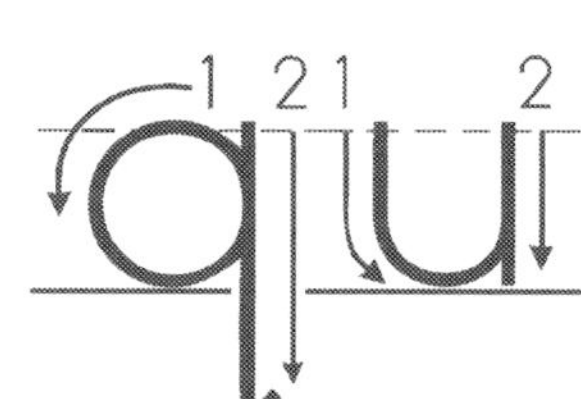

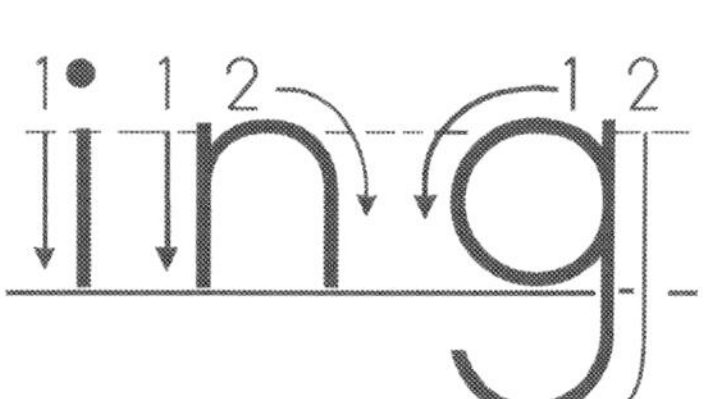

Q q Q q Q q

ing ing ing ing

Y y Y y Y y

qu qu qu qu qu qu

sing ring ding ping

who who who who

Who

whose

wing

finger

bring

going

queen

quiet

quick

quit

Trace and then copy

keeping

missing

eating

reading

sleeping

sitting

coming

looking

Who was

helping

playing

doing

giving

talking

Who is

taking

pushing

saving

living

Trace and then copy

school

beautiful

door

children

family

listen

world

because

always

woman

friend

flower

My story

Lesson 18

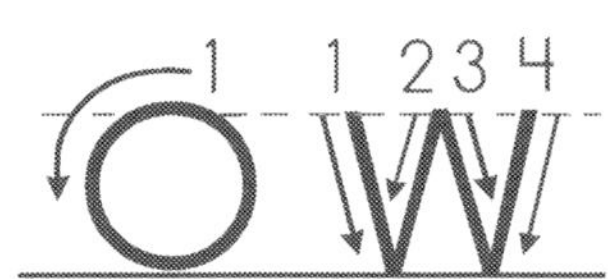

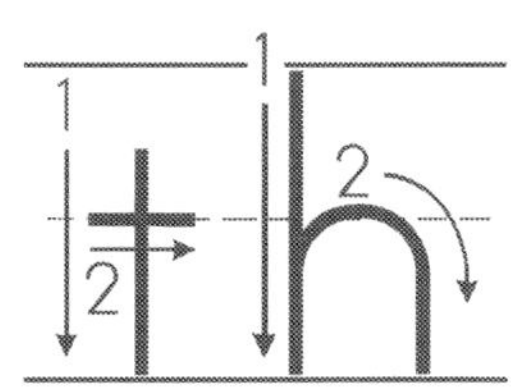

out loud about

shout stout sour

both mouth math

think round sound

now cow how wow

ground blouse mouse

Out

about

down

brown

both

smooth

three

cow

house

gown

Our town

Old tower

I am thin.

Very loud

that thing

one pound

that path

this month

Who is that?

Go slowly.

question

quick

thick

three

inside

outside

both doors

three cows

two eggs

Trace and then copy

Mouse ran in the house.

Tell me a story, please.

My house is beautiful.

Never go without me.

Who is down stairs?

That color is brown.

My story

Lesson 19

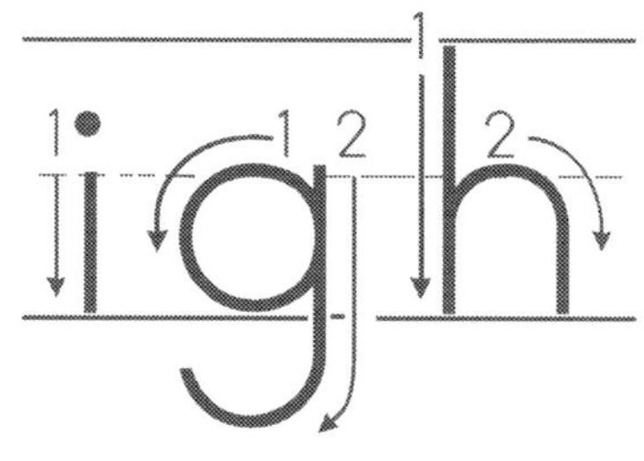

high might right

bright thigh light

few new dew blew

would would would

could could could

should should should

would

could

should

bring

string

now cow

few new

true blue

lighthouse

nightgown

You should

I could

We would

How loud?

New house

flew away

My teeth

Your tooth

white tiger

Who is it?

Thank you

I can read now.

Sit down here.

Go around it.

How loud was it?

The queen eats cake.

The birds flew away.

You should write this.

Go right or left.

I might go outside.

He should work hard.

She might do it quickly.

There should be light.

My story

Lesson 20

c g ph

face ice place

spice nice rice

price twice since

mice cent cage

phone giant gem

photo elephant

giant

brown rice

nice place

gentle

Grace

Never

always

ginger

ice cream

know

Just great

playing nice

since

pencil

never stops

rocket

space

page

baby

circus

Giggle Bunny

This is our kitchen.

I have a cell phone.

Once upon a time.

I know these people.

The door and the floor.

End of the writing lesson.

I am almost done.

Please wash your face.

A king and a queen

lived in a big castle.

They like to eat pizza.

All done. I will stop now.

My story

Copy this page for practice.

This is a downloadable program.

Giggle Bunny's READING LESSON is an animated program designed to be used with the Reading Lesson book. This interactive program with enchanting and fun host, Giggle Bunny, will teach your child to read the fun way.

The program closely follows the structure of the lessons in the book. With the help of lively animations, new sounds, letter combinations and words come alive. In every lesson, you will find Word Theater, games with trophies and typing practice. Entertaining Giggle Bunny makes it all a joy for the child.

The program can be purchased as a download at our website.

www.readinglesson.com

This is a downloadable program.

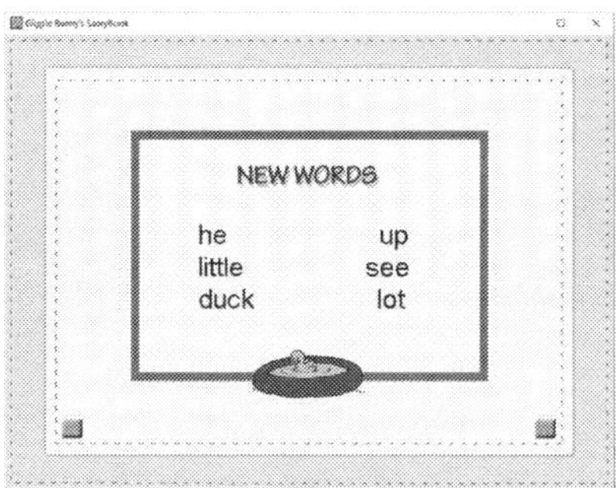

The StoryBook animated program contains 40 short stories. These stories reintroduce the words learned in the Reading Lesson to build vocabulary and fluency.

The stories are very simple at first and get longer and more complex as we go on. At the beginning of each story, there is a list of the new words. The words sound out when clicked and the phonic units are highlighted.

The animations are sweet and full of surprises. The pages are clean and the text is easy to read. Printable version of the stories is also included with the program. The child can print out the stories and make little books out of them. The StoryBook is a companion to the Reading Lesson but can also be used as a stand-alone program.

The program is available as a download at our website.

www.readinglesson.com